Shrubs for small gardens

Shrubs for small gardens

A Wisley handbook

Keith Rushforth

Cassell

The Royal Horticultural Society

Cassell Educational Limited
Artillery House, Artillery Row
London SW1P 1RT
for the Royal Horticultural Society

First published 1989

British Library Cataloguing in Publication Data

Rushforth, Keith D.
  Shrubs for small gardens.
  I. Gardens. Shrubs
  I. Title II. Series
  635.9′76

  ISBN 0–304–32198–2

Photographs by Michael Warren and the Harry Smith Collection
Design by Lesley Stewart
Phototypesetting by Chapterhouse, Formby
Printed in Hong Kong by Wing King Tong Co. Ltd

Contents

Introduction

This book is a guide to the use of shrubs in small gardens. It considers their role and placing in the garden, gives advice on purchase, planting and pruning and finally provides a selection of over 250 suitable shrubs.

Shrubs, if well chosen, have many merits, particularly where the small garden is concerned. Their attractions are not confined to flowers, but include colourful foliage and fruits, decorative bark and distinctive shapes or habits. They can supply interest throughout the seasons, often changing as the year progresses, and once established they require little maintenance, apart from any pruning which may be necessary. Although shrubs may seem expensive to buy, they are a good investment, lasting for at least five years and usually many more. They are also better value than most other plants, relative to the area of garden they occupy.

Shrubs give structure to a garden, associating well with anything from spring bulbs to herbaceous plants and acting as a backcloth to seasonal flowers. They have practical advantages as well, contributing shelter and shade to the garden, screening and separating different areas, filling surplus space and providing homes and food for wildlife.

The definition of a shrub is a low woody plant that does not grow as tall as a tree. For the purposes of this book, which is concerned with small gardens, a shrub can be defined as any woody plant in the height range of 4 in. to 10 ft (10 cm–3 m). Climbers are also included, being especially useful where ground space is scarce.

The size of garden envisaged in this book ranges from the small front and back gardens typical of many new housing estates – perhaps 15–20 by 30 ft (4.5–6 × 9 m) for the back garden – up to more generous plots 50 by 70 ft (15 × 21 m). Even if the overall dimensions of your garden are larger than these, there may still be small areas of garden at the front or side of the house and it is often useful to treat a large garden as a series of smaller spaces. At the other extreme, there is no minimum size of garden needed before shrubs can be introduced. Several of the smaller-growing shrubs can be used just as effectively in containers, such as tubs, half-barrels, old sinks or window boxes, as in a border or bed.

Opposite: the gracefully weeping *Buddleia alternifolia* makes a fine specimen shrub

The role of shrubs in a small garden

WHERE TO GROW SHRUBS

Shrubs can serve many different purposes, even in a small garden. They can be used individually as feature plants – at the edge of a lawn or patio, for instance, or beside a small pool; or they can form part of a mixed border, providing a background to the herbaceous element when it is at its best and giving substance to the border at other seasons. Dwarf shrubs lend interest and contrast to a rock garden; they may find a place in a raised bed or can be inserted in pockets of soil between the paving stones on a terrace. Dense low shrubs, like heathers and certain hebes, are useful as ground cover and some can be particularly valuable in a shady situation or on a slope which might otherwise be difficult to plant.

All sorts of shrubs are suitable for screening – to disguise a dull wall, break the outline of an ugly building or hide the vegetable plot. Many make excellent informal hedges and boundary-markers, especially those of naturally low growth. Although this type of hedge takes up more room than a closely clipped formal hedge, it offers the attractions of flowers and fruits, as well as foliage, and needs pruning only once a year or less. *Berberis × stenophylla*, *Hypericum* 'Hidcote' and *Potentilla fruticosa* are just some that can be recommended for the purpose.

Climbers and wall shrubs recommend themselves in a restricted space, where they can be grown up trellises, fences and walls and add another dimension to the garden. An effective boundary can be created with a climber such as ivy grown over a chain-link fence, making a natural feature that needs less room and maintenance than most hedges. Vigorous climbers can also be trained up trees to give a "second flowering", for example, a summer-flowering clematis grown through a magnolia. As already mentioned, shrubs can also be grown in containers to enliven a patio or small courtyard.

CHOOSING SHRUBS

Because space is limited in a small garden, there will only be room for a finite number of shrubs. Accordingly, careful thought should be given to their selection. The main requirement is that they represent good value for the space they occupy. The criteria for

Above: the cut-leaved Japanese maple, *Acer palmatum* 'Dissectum', provides a long season of interest with its elegant foliage

Below: *Berberis* × *stenophylla* (left) can be used as a delightful informal hedge; *Hedera algeriensis* 'Gloire de Marengo' (right) trained up an old tree stump

choosing any shrub should include not just its obvious attractions of flowers, fruit or foliage, but also its shape, the height and spread it will attain, and how quickly, the pruning and maintenance that will be necessary and its suitability for your conditions, particularly for the position in which you intend to place it. (Information on a wide range of shrubs and their individual needs is given in the final chapter, pp.34–62.) Do not include too many different kinds of shrub in a small garden, as the result will be fussy and cluttered.

GARDEN DESIGN WITH SHRUBS

Correct placing of a shrub or group of shrubs within the garden requires consideration of several factors, namely the scale of the setting, the shape or habit of plant which is appropriate to the setting and the use of foliage, flower and other characteristics within the setting.

Scale

The scale of planting is very important in creating an attractive garden. Scale, however, is a relative term and depends upon the constraints of the site. In a heather bed, for example, the plants are generally flat and low; here scale can be provided with a dwarf conifer or a miniature rowan, *Sorbus reducta*, to break up the monotony and thereby compliment the heathers. At the same time, scale must relate to the surroundings so that the whole planting, not just the individual shrubs, fits in with the space around. Thus, a broad expanse of lawn with a bed of low-growing shrubs at the far end will look odd if these abut the rear garden wall; instead, the planting should lead into or disguise the wall with taller shrubs. A shrub as a focal point in a long narrow garden would generally need to be tall and upright, whereas in a short but broad garden a spreading low shrub would be better balanced.

For obvious reasons, low-growing plants are usually placed at the front of a border, with tall ones at the back. However, nothing looks worse than orderly rows of plants based strictly on height and a better effect can be achieved by planting in informal drifts of varying heights. It may also be visually interesting to have an area of low plants between taller ones, so that the low group can be seen as a feature from one specific point in the garden. Scale is determined by function as well: space might suggest shrubs no taller than 5 ft (1.5 m) for a particular corner, but the need to screen the patio from a neighbour's window or draw the eye away from some distant monstrosity may dictate shrubs of twice that height.

Shape or habit

Shrubs are available in a multitude of shapes, each of which has a part to play in the garden. Three distinctive shapes are discussed below, with suggestions for their use.

Erect-growing or spiky shrubs, such as *Camellia* x *williamsii*, *Daphne mezereum*, *Hedera helix* 'Conglomerata Erecta' and *Mahonia* x *media*, are useful specimen plants on their own or can give height at the back of a border or provide a contrast to rounded or weeping shrubs. Many of them can also be trained against a wall.

Mound-forming or arching shrubs strike a restful note. Again, they can be used as individual specimens, perhaps at the edge of a pool or lawn, or included in a border, with the position dependent upon their size. Some may be effective cascading over a low wall. Examples in this category are *Ceanothus impressus*, *Cytisus* x *praecox*, *Exochorda* x *macrantha* 'The Bride', *Genista lydia*, *Arundinaria murieliae*, *Buddleia alternifolia* and *Chamaecyparis pisifera* 'Filifera Aurea'.

Low spreading shrubs, like heathers, *Juniperus horizontalis*, *Rhododendron* 'Elisabeth Hobbie' and *R. impeditum*, can be used *en masse* to create an illusion of space. They are excellent for carpeting the ground between taller shrubs and trees or at the front of a border and can help to unify different parts of a small garden.

Shape should always be considered in design, but take care not to over-use the contrasting shapes or they will lose their impact and produce a restless effect. This is particularly true in a small garden, where the essential element of surprise will disappear if more than one or two contrasting plants are used.

When positioning shrubs, it is important to consider their future growth in spread as well as height and to allow them room for development. This will mean planting them some distance apart in a border, which will look very sparse to begin with, although the gaps can be filled with annuals, bulbs and other temporary plants in the early years.

Foliage, flowers, fruit and bark

Most shrubs are chosen for their flowers or foliage and, to a lesser extent, their fruit or bark, since these are the features which catch the eye in the garden centre or in a nursery catalogue. Although

Above: the fragrant flowers of *Daphne mezereum* are welcome in early spring

Below: *Ceanothus* 'Blue Mound' forms a dense dome of evergreen foliage covered with blue flowers in May and June

Above: many of the brooms, like *Cytisus* × *kewensis*, are effective at the edge of a low wall

Below: the dwarf *Rhododendron impeditum* gives attractive groundcover

we are all susceptible to the attractions of flowers, floral beauty should not be the sole criterion in choosing a shrub, particularly for a small garden, where it is important that plants should earn their keep and perform for as long as possible. Rather, consider what the whole shrub has to offer and try to see the flowers as the icing on a well-conceived cake, with scale, habit and foliage forming the framework of the overall planting. Foliage, after all, is there for the whole summer in most plants and all the year in evergreens, flowers but for a few days or weeks.

Many shrubs have small leaves, for instance, *Escallonia*, *Hebe* and *Osmanthus*. These dainty-leaved plants are generally the most peaceful, with the mass of foliage providing a background to their own and other flowers and creating a feeling of space, which is especially welcome in a small garden. Shrubs with bolder or larger leaves have an architectural quality, which makes them stand out at a distance, and thus they tend to reduce space so that an area becomes more intimate. Examples include *Viburnum davidii*, with big simple leaves, *Nandina domestica*, with leaves composed of small leaflets, and *Paeonia delavayi*, with deeply dissected leaves. Shrubs with distinctive leaves have a place in the small garden, as accent plants in a mixed border or as impressive features on their own, but they should not be overdone.

Shrubs with evergreen foliage are useful for providing permanent interest. They also make a good backcloth for the display of winter flowers, such as those of *Lonicera fragrantissima*, and supply privacy and shelter. However, all evergreen foliage becomes too dark at some seasons and can be oppressive if there is too much of it. The best effect is when perhaps a quarter to a third of the total number of shrubs is evergreen and these should be distributed throughout the garden rather than forming a solid block.

Variegated shrubs, which have silvery, white or golden margins, splashes or mottlings on the leaves, can help to enliven or break up a planting scheme. *Elaeagnus* × *ebbingei* 'Gilt Edge' is a well-known example. Again, avoid over-using variegated foliage in a small garden and remember that different types of variegation rarely combine well.

There are many shrubs with coloured, as opposed to green leaves, ranging from the copper of *Acer palmatum* 'Bloodgood' and the yellow of *Berberis thunbergii* 'Aurea' to the glaucous-blue of *Abies lasiocarpa* 'Compacta' and the silvery white of *Artemisia* 'Powis Castle'. Grey and silver-leaved shrubs are especially

Opposite: the yellow leaves of *Berberis thunbergii* 'Aurea' brighten a dark corner

valuable as a foil for other colours. The more strikingly coloured shrubs can be difficult to place and often look better as individual specimens or associated with green- or grey-foliaged plants rather than with each other. Purple-leaved shrubs should be used with particular care if they are not to overwhelm, although they can be lightened with variegated plants.

In several shrubs, the coloured new foliage is an attraction, as with *Pieris formosa* 'Wakehurst' and *Photinia* × *fraseri* 'Red Robin'. In many more, the dying autumn leaves develop beautiful tints, for instance, deciduous azaleas and *Acer palmatum* 'Dissectum', contributing a further dimension to the garden at that time of year. As a bonus, the leaves of a few shrubs, such as *Olearia macrodonta*, release a pleasant aroma, usually when crushed.

A garden without the varied colours, shapes and scents of flowers would be a dull place. There is no doubt that these are the chief attraction of the majority of shrubs and the most conspicuous feature when they are out, even though they are relatively fleeting. In a small garden, shrubs which produce a protracted display, such as *Camellia* × *williamsii*, with a succession of individual blooms, and *Hydrangea paniculata*, with unusually long-lasting flowers, are especially desirable. By careful selection, it is possible to have a shrub in flower every month of the year. Winter-flowering shrubs are always appreciated and many of them, like *Mahonia* × *media*, fill the air with their rich perfume.

Several shrubs have decorative fruit, which is also valuable in the autumn and winter period and sometimes at other seasons. The silky seedheads of *Clematis alpina* 'Frances Rivis' and the large hips of *Rosa rugosa* 'Fru Dagmar Hastrup', for example, both appear from July on, while the berries of some cotoneasters persist until Easter. Bark is largely a winter feature, being hidden by foliage at other times. It is best displayed when the shrub is cut back hard in early spring, as with the forms of *Cornus alba*, in which the one-year-old twigs are brightly coloured. The peeling bark of shrubs like *Cistus laurifolius* and *Weigela middendorffiana* is also attractive.

Shrubs grown for winter effect, whether bark, fruit or flowers, should be placed where they can be seen from inside or near the front door or a much-used path if they are scented, otherwise they may easily be missed until you venture out into the garden again in spring!

Above: 'St Ewe', one of the many valuable *Camellia × williamsii* forms, flowers over a long period

Below: *Spiraea japonica* 'Gold Flame' has delicately coloured young foliage

Above: the brilliantly coloured berries of *Pernettya mucronata* 'Cherry Ripe' remain throughout the winter

Below: the dogwoods, such as *Cornus stolonifera* 'Flaviramea', make a striking contribution to the winter scene

Practical considerations

Successful gardening involves knowing the limitations of your site, as well as its good points, and taking these into account when planning and planting. Not all shrubs like or tolerate the same conditions and an appreciation of their individual preferences can make the difference between a garden where you have time to sit back and enjoy the display and one where every blossom is gained only after a marathon effort. (Guidance on soil, light, hardiness, pruning and any other requirements is given in the selection of shrubs, pp.34–62.) This chapter looks at the factors affecting your choice of shrubs, with particular reference to the problems associated with small gardens.

SOIL

Very few gardens possess the ideal soil – a good loam – and the type of soil may place a constraint upon what will grow or reduce its rate of growth. Fortunately, most shrubs are accommodating plants, only a small number having definite dislikes, and it is possible to find a shrub to suit almost every soil.

Rhododendrons and many heathers and their relatives will not grow on soils derived from chalk or limestone. Giving nutrients in a chelated form may assist where the soil is only slightly alkaline, but in the long run it is better to choose from the many shrubs which grow freely on these soils rather than struggle to get healthy rhododendrons. Similarly, acid soils impose restrictions on what will succeed and, although they can be improved by liming, it is wiser to select from the numerous shrubs available which thrive in such soils.

Clay soils are difficult for shrubs to root through and poorly drained. They also tend to take time to warm up in spring, causing plants to be late in starting into growth and slow to grow, especially when young. They can be improved by working in organic matter and by digging them in autumn to let frost break down the clods. Surface water should be drained away with pipes, or the border shaped into mounds to give sufficient rooting depth. Avoid walking on clay soils when they are wet, as this destroys the structure, reducing it to a formless mass which is impenetrable to plant roots.

Sandy soils, by contrast, are very free-draining, drying out quickly in the summer, and hold little in the way of nutrients,

although plants can root readily through them. They can be improved by adding organic matter, such as peat or well-rotted manure, which will increase their capacity for retaining water and nutrients.

Problems of the soil, or lack of it, are common in small gardens. Many town gardens suffer from dry impoverished soil, particularly where there is heavy shade. Thorough preparation of the soil, by digging and incorporating plenty of humus is essential. Compaction, which prevents roots penetrating the soil and water draining away, is often found in new gardens where heavy machinery has been used during house construction. Sometimes the whole layer of topsoil may have been removed as well. Digging to two spade depths (see p.26) is the most practical method to relieve compaction in a small garden and it may also be necessary to buy in extra top soil.

Closely packed soil may lead to waterlogging or very wet conditions, which few plants can survive. Installing drainage is the best way to improve such a soil, but it will only work if there is somewhere for the water to drain away. If this is not possible, plant on mounds or choose shrubs like Cornus alba that will tolerate wetness.

CLIMATE

Although there is considerable variation in climate over the length of Britain, it is surprising how many shrubs will thrive throughout the country. However, some shrubs are only reliably hardy in the milder parts of southern and western Britain. This applies to many hebes, for example and there is little point trying them in colder districts unless they can be given suitable protection. Other shrubs, lilac, for instance, do better in the eastern counties, although they will grow elsewhere. Town gardens usually benefit from higher temperatures in winter than the suburbs and countryside, owing to the heat escaping from houses and offices. As a result, less hardy shrubs can often be grown, especially against walls, and camellias are particularly successful in towns.

Like camellias, a number of shrubs are vulnerable to late spring frosts, either because the flowers are pre-formed in buds made the previous year or because they have early flowers whose petals are easily damaged. If the new growth is injured by frost, that season's flowering may be lost. Shrubs of this kind (noted in the

Opposite: Syringa microphylla 'Superba' and other lilacs will thrive on alkaline soils

Above: the magnificent *Desfontainea spinosa* does best in warm moist conditions and lime-free soil

Below: the Mexican orange blossom, *Choisya ternata*, is tough enough for seaside gardens

last chapter, pp.34–62, as needing some protection) should be positioned in the garden so that they are not in frost pockets and, if possible, sheltered from the early morning sun to reduce the risk of damage. The alternatives are either to choose frost-hardier shrubs, or to accept the fact that every now and then frost might mar the display.

Exposure to winds influences the growth rate and appearance of all plants, not only causing physical damage but also drying out the foliage and soil. Turbulence from buildings is a frequent problem in towns. Planting a windbreak or making a screen can be a solution, if there is room. Otherwise, tough plants, such as *Cornus alba*, *Cotinus coggygria*, *Euonymus fortunei* cultivars, *Hydrangea paniculata*, heathers and *Pernettya mucronata*, should be chosen where wind exposure is severe.

Coastal gardens tend to be windier than those inland, with nothing to reduce the wind speed as it comes off the sea, and salt spray adds to the damage. In these situations, it is advisable to select salt-resistant shrubs, which include *Choisya ternata*, *Cotoneaster*, *Cytisus*, *Escallonia*, *Euonymus*, *Hebe*, *Olearia*, *Rhamnus alaterna* and *Senecio*.

ASPECT

Shrubs vary in their light requirements. Many grow best in an open sunny position, where they receive from four to six hours daily of direct sunlight in summer (described as "sun" in the list of shrubs, pp.34–62). A small number need more sun, really wanting a hot dry site with as much sunlight as possible in our climate (noted as "full sun" in the list). These are mainly members of the pea family, such as *Genista* and *Cytisus*, and can be useful in small enclosed gardens where there is often a hot dry spot, perhaps at the foot of a south-facing wall.

Other shrubs tolerate or prefer light shade, where they receive less than four hours direct sunlight each day; an open north-facing bed or wall would be in this category. Permanent heavy shade, which is a common feature in small gardens overlooked by taller buildings or trees, is more difficult to deal with. Nevertheless, there are several shrubs such as *Mahonia* × *media*, *Viburnum davidii* and *Euonymus fortunei*, that will accept deep shade.

Choosing the right shrub for the level of shade is important: those needing full sun will be weedy and at best flower very poorly if in shade, whereas many shade-loving shrubs, like some rhododendrons, will not be happy in full sun. (See also the Wisley handbook, *Plants for shade*.)

Above: the distinctive flowers of *Ribes speciosum*, borne in April and May, are vulnerable to late frosts

Below: *Convolvulus cneorum*, a charming small shrub for a hot dry position

Purchase and planting

TYPES OF SHRUB AVAILABLE

Shrubs are usually purchased as bare-rooted, root-balled or container-grown plants. Bare-rooted shrubs are grown in open fields in a nursery and, when they are lifted, all the soil is shaken off; the roots are then wrapped in some material, such as damp straw, to prevent then drying out. Many deciduous shrubs may be bought bare-rooted, for planting during the winter season from November until March. Because they are grown in the field, larger sizes are often available.

Evergreens rarely survive with bare roots, but can be moved with a root ball, which involves keeping the soil attached to the roots and wrapping them in hessian. Root-balled shrubs can be planted out earlier in the autumn and into April.

Container-grown shrubs are put into a pot one or more years before being sold. As a result, they should not suffer any check from loss of roots on lifting and can be planted at times other than during the winter planting season. Most shrubs from garden centres are container-grown for this reason, allowing them to be sold and planted at any time of the year. Another advantage is that evergreens and shrubs with thick fleshy roots, such as magnolias, can be planted more safely if container-grown, even during the winter.

The main risk with a container-grown shrub is that it may have become pot-bound and, when planted, will not form a satisfactory new root system in the different environment of the soil. This can happen when the shrub has spent too long in a container and the roots are growing round the pot, which they will continue to do, rather than spreading out into the soil. Container-grown shrubs are also more expensive than bare-rooted plants and in hard winters the roots can be killed in the containers, leading to failure in the spring.

BUYING SHRUBS

Shrubs can be purchased from reputable nurseries by mail order (or in person), from garden centres and from plant sales areas attached to gardens open to the public, the latter often stocking more unusual shrubs. Generally, bare-rooted shrubs should be bought and planted only during the period November to early

The popular *Magnolia stellata* carries a profusion of flowers in March and April

March, while container-grown shrubs can be bought at other times. However, it is wise to avoid the midsummer months, July and early August, when they will be growing vigorously and a lot of attention to watering will be necessary. Slightly tender shrubs are best planted in late spring; for other shrubs, autumn planting is usually preferable, but not always as convenient.

PLANTING

Planting will vary a little according to whether you are making a new bed or border or replacing plants in an existing one. With a new bed, the outline should be marked out and perennial weeds should be killed with a herbicide like glyphosate, which does not persist in the soil, taking care to avoid any cultivated plants. This is best carried out in September, but can be done at any time when the weeds are actively growing. Once the weeds are dead, the ground should be well dug, or dug to two spade depths if there is any sign of soil compaction (the top spit of soil is removed and put to one side and then the second spit is turned over with a spade before replacing the topsoil). Autumn is the recommended time for digging, especially on heavy soils, and the soil can be left over winter to let the action of frost break it down. Organic matter, such as peat or well-rotted manure, can be spread over the bed before digging and thus incorporated.

The first stage in planting is to excavate a hole, which should be dug at least 4 in. (10 cm) larger in each direction than the spread of the shrub's roots or the size of the container. If planting into an existing bed, the bottom and sides of the hole should be forked over, so that the roots can easily grow out. Soil should then be placed back in the hole until it is as deep as the depth of the roots, but no deeper. Peat or potting compost can be mixed with the soil and this is advisable for container-grown shrubs, as the compost in the pot will contain peat. Do not attempt to plant if the ground is frozen solid or covered with snow, but keep the shrub in a cool place until the weather is suitable.

The roots of a bare-rooted shrub should be spread out in the hole and soil worked between them, consolidating it in layers with the feet, but being careful not to stamp on the roots. The final soil level should be at the nursery soil level, which will show as a dark mark on the stems or bark. If some roots are badly damaged, the damaged parts can be cut out, but as far as possible avoid further reducing the roots.

Before planting a container-grown shrub, give it a good soak in a bucket of water for five to ten minutes. This is especially important when planting in summer, but even in mid-winter the compost in a container can easily dry out. Bare-rooted plants will also benefit from a brief soaking if they are dry. With a container-grown shrub, the roots may be circling the bottom of the pot and they should either be teased out or the surface spiral of roots cut at three points, cutting no deeper into the compost than $\frac{3}{4}$ in. (1 cm), so that new spreading roots are formed. If the plant is pot-bound, with very woody circling roots, it should be returned to the supplier. Then proceed as with a bare-rooted shrub, again planting no deeper than the soil surface level of the container.

Root-balled shrubs should be placed in the hole and the hessian untied and cut away at the sides. Do not attempt to remove it from beneath the root ball, or you will damage this and reduce its effectiveness; the hessian will rot away.

After planting, the shrub should be watered, using at least 2 gallons (9 litres) water per plant. In late spring and summer, the same amount of water will have to be given once a week or more for a month and you should keep an eye open for any sign of wilting. A few days after planting and after windy weather, check that the soil around the roots has not been loosened and firm it if necessary. Most shrubs will not require any staking, but if they do, bamboo canes should be used, attaching the shrub to the cane with tape.

Maintenance

WEED CONTROL

The first requirement with any newly planted shrub is to get it to grow strongly. Provided proper care has been taken with the actual planting, this is best achieved by thorough weed control for at least the first two seasons after planting. Grasses and clovers are the worst weeds from the point of view of their effect upon shrubs, since they compete fiercely for water and nutrients. Other broad-leaved weeds are much less of a problem, although they can be very unsightly. Spring bulbs and annuals can be used to fill the gaps between shrubs and are unlikely to harm them, but vigorous ground-covering perennials like *Geranium* should be avoided for the first couple of seasons.

Starting with a weed-free bed (see p.26) is essential to satisfactory weed control. Subsequent weed invasion is best controlled by using a long-lasting mulch. Composted conifer bark is highly recommended for the purpose and will last for three to five years. It is available in bags from garden centres or sometimes in bulk at a lower price from local landscape contractors. Peat and other forms of organic matter can also be used, but do not persist as long. In certain situations, pea gravel, around ¾ in. (1 cm) in diameter, can make a very satisfactory mulch. Sheeting materials, such as 500 gauge black polythene, are very effective too, although unattractive in a garden. However, porous sheeting materials can be useful as a layer beneath the mulch to prevent it being worked into the soil – even gravel becomes incorporated into the soil by the action of worms. Some mulches can be helpful in providing food, particularly manure, spent hops and mushroom compost. The latter has a high pH and is therefore unsuitable for acid-loving shrubs. Peat and bark do not add nutrients, although all organic mulches will increase the humus content of the soil and help to improve its structure.

A mulch must be spread thickly enough to prevent weeds germinating through it, to a depth of at least 2 in. (5 cm) and preferably 4 in. (10 cm) (except with sheet materials). The ground should be free of perennial weeds, such as couch grass and ground elder, before the mulch is laid; these are best killed with glyphosate. The mulch is best applied in spring, when the ground is moist and is beginning to warm up.

Herbicides are another method of controlling weeds in beds

With shiny evergreen leaves, fragrant flowers and bright red berries,
Skimmia japonica 'Foremanii' has everything to recommend it

and borders. They include foliage-acting weedkillers, like glyphosate, and soil-acting ones, like simazine or dichlobenil, which
give season-long control. Always take particular care not to over-
dose and to avoid the chemicals coming in contact with the
shrubs or other ornamental plants. When using herbicides, follow
the recommendations given by the manufacturer on the label.
(See also the Wisley handbook, *Weed control in the garden*.)

WATERING

Weed control and mulching will reduce the need for watering, by
limiting competition for moisture and by restricting water loss
through evaporation from the soil. However, in very dry periods
and with newly planted shrubs, some extra watering may be
necessary. Potentially, a shrub bed can lose the equivalent of
roughly 1 in. (2.5 cm) of rainfall a week during June and July, $\frac{3}{4}$ in.
(2 cm) in May and August and $\frac{1}{2}$ in. (1 cm) in April and September.
If there has not been this amount of rain, the missing water should
be replaced, preferably with a sprinkler applied to the whole bed.

Hibiscus syriacus 'Diana' (left), a recently introduced form from the USA; the calico bush, *Kalmia latifolia* (right), flourishes in the same conditions as rhododendrons

FEEDING

In most garden situations, shrubs will not require feeding, although it may enhance growth. Well-rotted manure or compost can be used as part of the mulch or as a top dressing, or a chemical fertilizer can be applied. Do not over-feed, as this may poison the shrubs. A general-purpose fertilizer, with an analysis of around 7 to 10 parts each of nitrogen, phosphorus and potassium, is suitable, at a rate of 2 oz per square yard (70 gm per m²). With all shrubs, it is especially important to apply any feed to bare earth. If grass or other weeds are present, they and not the shrub will make the increased growth, which could lead to a reduction in the growth of the shrub owing to the competition.

PESTS AND DISEASES

Although shrubs can be affected by a variety of pests and diseases, these are seldom serious. Aphids, which may occasionally be a problem, can be easily controlled with a proprietary insecticide, if possible using one which does not kill ladybirds and other insect predators of aphids. Fungal diseases, such as honey fungus, caused by species of *Armillaria*, can be extremely damaging and, if symptoms are suspected, it is wise to seek expert advice. (For further information, see the *Collins Guide to the Pests, Diseases and Disorders of Garden Plants* by Stefan Buczacki and Keith Harris.)

Pruning

Pruning has three main objectives – to control the size and shape of a shrub, to keep it healthy and to enhance its beauty.

CONTROL AND SHAPING

Pruning to control size is necessary when a shrub is growing too large for its location. The aim is to reduce its size without just hacking it back; if the offending branches are simply lopped off, regrowth is likely to be more vigorous and may quickly cause as much trouble as the portion removed. Prune by cutting the longer branches back to a suitable and smaller sideshoot, which will retain the original shape of the shrub and keep it in a flowering and fruiting stage.

When shrubs are seriously overgrown, pruning back to side branches may not be sufficient and they may respond to being coppiced, that is, cut down to near ground level. This technique may also be effective at invigorating those in poor health (although if a fungal disease at the roots is the reason for the condition, it is unlikely to be successful). With most shrubs, the new growth made after coppicing is unlikely to flower for two to three years. This hard pruning should normally be carried out in the dormant season or after flowering for deciduous shrubs and in early spring for evergreens like camellias.

MAINTAINING HEALTH

Pruning for health is a matter of removing weak, damaged, dead or overcrowded shoots, in order to prevent or restrict the entry of disease and to eliminate places where damaging insects can hide. Promptly remove any dying branch as soon as it is noticed, by cutting it off at the base. Any branches which are crossing or rubbing together should also be removed. Suckers on grafted shrubs (representing the rootstock, not the desired form) should be removed at their point of origin. With suckers from the roots, the simplest method is to pull the sucker while levering a spade between it and the stem. On variegated shrubs, branches sometimes revert to pure green and these too should be cut out before they take over.

Above: flowering on the previous season's shoots, *Buddleia globosa* (left) and *Clematis alpina* 'Frances Rivis' (right) may be pruned after flowering

Below: Deutzias, like *D.* × *rosea* 'Carminea', are best pruned every three or four years

ENHANCING BEAUTY

The method and timing of pruning for decorative effect will vary, depending upon how the flowers or other attractive features, such as leaves or bark, are produced. Deciduous shrubs can be divided into two categories – those which flower on last summer's shoots and those which flower on the current season's shoots. Knowing to which group a shrub belongs is important, since different species in one genus may respond very differently. For example, *Buddleia globosa* and *Clematis alpina* are in the first category, while *Buddleia davidii* and *Clematis vernayi* are in the second.

Shrubs flowering on shoots grown last year should be pruned immediately after flowering, which is generally in spring and early summer. The older shoots are removed at the point of origin, encouraging young shoots to replace them in the framework of the bush. The number of young shoots may need to be thinned out at the same time to keep the shrub compact. Many shrubs in this class, for instance *Deutzia* and *Kolkwitzia*, actually flower better on the spur shoots produced on three- or four-year-old shoots; in their case, the pruning regime should be to remove shoots every three or four years. If the fruits as well as the flowers are a feature, as in *Berberis* × *stenophylla*, prune the shrub more lightly.

Shrubs which flower on the current season's shoots are mostly summer- and early autumn-flowering and can be hard pruned in March to give a better display later. Examples are *Buddleia davidii*, *Ceratostigma willmottianum*, *Hypericum* 'Hidcote' and *Indigofera heterantha*. If left unpruned, they will usually flower earlier in the summer, but with smaller blooms.

Shrubs like *Cornus alba*, which are grown for the strongly coloured bark of the one-year-old shoots, and some foliage shrubs, such as *Artemisia*, can be treated in the same way to make the most of their attractive features.

Evergreen shrubs, on the whole, require no pruning, except to remove any damaged growth or reverted shoots and to keep them trim and shapely. This should be carried out in late May or early June.

Many other shrubs will give an attractive display without regular pruning, although they will benefit from the removal of dead, diseased or overcrowded shoots. (For further guidance, see the Wisley handbook, *Pruning ornamental shrubs*.)

A selection of shrubs for small gardens

This chapter contains brief descriptions of over 250 shrubs suitable for small gardens. Most of them have been selected on the basis that they are reliable in gardens throughout the British Isles and are readily available from local garden centres or from the larger national nurseries; a few are less common or may need some extra attention. In many cases, the featured shrub is one of several similar plants and it is only possible to mention one or two of them, as for example with the numerous forms of *Camellia* × *williamsii*. Space does not allow discussion of more than a sample of available shrubs and the final selection inevitably has a personal bias. However, all have been chosen for their value in a small garden and their ability to contribute something more than just a short burst of bloom.

The information given for each shrub includes its likely height and spread after ten years, in average conditions, what aspect it prefers and any special requirements such as soil or pruning; where there is no reference to these, it can be assumed that any soil is suitable and that no pruning is necessary. If the shrub is evergreen, this is noted, otherwise it is deciduous.

The shrubs, including climbers, are grouped according to their flowering season, from early spring to late summer, followed by sections on autumn and winter effect and year-round interest. All have been selected for more than one attribute and there is therefore some overlap of categories, with many of the flowering shrubs having attractive foliage or fruits and vice-versa. (For further information about particular groups, see the following titles in the Wisley handbook series – *Climbing and wall plants*; *Ground cover plants*; *Camellias*; *Clematis*; *Heaths and heathers*; *Rhododendrons* and *Roses*. A companion volume to this, *Trees for small gardens*, may also be of interest.)

EARLY SPRING FLOWERS – LATE FEBRUARY TO EARLY APRIL

Abeliophyllum distichum Bare twigs covered with pale bluish pink flowers scented of almonds. Plant against a south- or west-facing wall in sun. Grows to 5 ft (1.5 m) tall and wide. Prune by removing old shoots after flowering.
Camellia × **williamsii** Large evergreen shrub, 10–16½ by 6½ ft (3–5 × 2 m), but can be controlled by pruning after flowering. Preferable to the more usual C. *japonica*,

Above: *Chaemomeles* × *superba* 'Pink Lady' (left), with its spreading horizontal branches, is particularly suitable for a wall; *Corylopsis pauciflora* (right) flowers reliably each year, in the right situation, and deserves to be more widely grown

as the cerise-pink flowers are carried in successive flushes from February until May, are more frost-hardy and drop the petals once over. Will grow in full sun but better in light shade. Avoid alkaline soils. 'Donation', semi-double flowers. 'St Ewe', single but effective flowers (see p.17).

Chaenomeles × superba (japonica)   Good for walls or open ground, forming a dense domed bush, 3–5 by 5 ft (1–1.5 × 1.5 m). Flowering from March into May, followed by edible "quince" fruits. Prune after flowering to remove old wood. Sun or light shade. 'Crimson and Gold', crimson petals and contrasting gold anthers. 'Knaphill Scarlet', large, brilliant red flowers. 'Pink Lady', flowers crimson in bud, opening to rose-pink.

Corylopsis pauciflora   Scented primrose-yellow flowers on bare branches in March. Makes a rounded bush, 3–5 by 3 ft (1–1.5 × 1 m). Site to protect from early morning sun and wind.

Daphne mezereum (mezereon)   Purplish red, fragrant flowers along erect branches, succeeded by poisonous red berries in July. A short-lived bush, 3 by 2 ft (1 × 0.6 m). Full sun to light shade. Any moist soil (see p.12).

D. odora 'Aureomarginata'   Evergreen with leaves margined creamy white, forming rounded bush, 4 by 5 ft (1.2 × 1.5 m). Flowers fragrant, purplish red. Sun or light shade.

Rhododendron   All require acid soil rich in organic matter; never plant deeply and mulch with peat, leafmould or conifer bark. Larger growing sorts should be dead-headed, removing faded flowers before seed is set, to encourage next season's blooms. Dwarf kinds will take full sun if the soil is sufficiently moist, taller ones are better in dappled shade.

R. pemakoense   Develops into a very dense, low, evergreen bush, 1 by 2 ft (0.3 × 0.6 m), with small, dark green leaves. Flowers single or in pairs, completely covering the plant. Place where early morning sun will not catch it, as the flowers are tender.

Spiraea thunbergii   Twiggy bush, 3–5 by 5 ft (1–1.5 × 1.5 m), with arching habit. Small, pure white flowers on leafless twigs, followed by fresh green, new foliage. Full sun (see p.36).

Above: the well-known *Spiraea thunbergii* succeeds in ordinary soil and a sunny spot

Below: *Berberis darwinii* will grow on chalky soils

Stachyurus chinensis Grows to 6 by 6½ ft (1.8 × 2 m). Cup-shaped pale yellow flowers hang beneath arching leafless shoots. Sun or light shade. 'Magpie', grey-green leaves margined with cream and with a rose-coloured tinge.

LATE SPRING FLOWERS – APRIL TO MAY

Berberis candidula Dense dome-shaped evergreen, 2½ by 3 ft (0.8 × 1 m). Glossy green leaves with a silver-blue reverse and solitary, bright yellow flowers succeeded by purple-black berries. Full sun to light shade.

B. darwinii Spectacular when in full flower, with short drooping clusters of 10 to 12 blossoms, in bud deep reddish orange, opening to deep yellow. Berries plum-coloured with waxy coating in autumn, often accompanied by a second small flush of bloom. Evergreen, having deep glossy green leaves with three small prickles. Upright habit, usually up to 5 ft (1.8 m) high, but occasionally taller, by 6½ ft (2 m). Responds to pruning. Full sun or light shade. Can be damaged by severe cold in exposed situations.

B. × stenophylla Evergreen narrow-leaved shrub, 6½–10 ft (2–3 m) high, with graceful habit. Golden yellow flowers carried beneath the arching branches of last season's growth, followed by massed blue-purple fruits. Makes a very effective semi-formal hedge. Trimmed once a year after flowering, new growths will be 2–3 ft (0.6–1 m) long and will flower next spring. Full sun or light shade (see p.9).

Ceanothus (Californian lilac) The spring-flowering kinds, usually evergreen (as are those below), require very little pruning. Should be given a sheltered sunny position, many being recommended as wall shrubs, and will not flourish on shallow soils over chalk.

C. 'A.T. Johnson' Grows 5–10 ft (1.5–3 m) tall. Rich blue flowers borne in both spring and autumn.

C. impressus Low spreading plant, 3–5 ft (1–1.5 m) high and across, with deep blue flowers which smother the small veined leaves.

C. thyrsiflorus var. repens Hardy variety which retains a low prostrate shape, ultimately 3 by 6½–10 ft (1 × 2–3 m). Mid-blue flowers, set off by glossy foliage.

Choisya ternata (Mexican orange blossom) Slow-growing evergreen, 10–13 ft (3–4 m) high, but will withstand cutting back. Leaves consist of three leaflets and are aromatic if crushed. White flowers strongly scented of orange blossom, carried mainly in spring and autumn. Prune to control shape and lightly after the spring flush of flowers for better autumn blossom. Full sun to light shade. Needs a sheltered position in cold districts (see p.22). 'Sundance', with golden foliage, promises to be smaller growing and is best in light shade.

Clematis alpina 'Frances Rivis' Low climber, 6½ by 6½–13 ft (2 × 2–4 m), with violet-blue flowers and deeply divided leaves. The silky seedheads are attractive from July on. Prune only to control spread, since flowers are formed on last season's shoots. Sun or light shade (see p.32).

Cytisus (broom) Short-lived but very floriferous, with pea-like flowers. They grow in all well-drained soils, but must have full sun. The small leaves are soon lost and slender green twigs give the effect of leaves. Brooms do not like any pruning, although shoots can be shortened successfully if they are still green below the point of the cut.

C. × beanii Deep golden yellow flowers in sprays up to 12 in. (30 cm) long from last year's growths. A low semi-prostrate plant, 1½ by 3–5 ft (1–1.5 m). Best replaced every three to four years (see p.38).

C. × kewensis Procumbent shrub, 8 in. by 5 ft (20 cm × 1.5 m), with creamy yellow flowers (see p.13).

C. × praecox Flowers rich cream to sulphur-yellow. Mounded habit with arching shoots, 3–5 ft by 5–6½ ft (1–1.5 × 1.5–2 m).

A superb combination of deep yellow *Cytisus* × *beanii* and purple aubrieta (left) at the National Trust property, Polesden Lacey, in Surrey; the fast-growing *Daphne* × *burkwoodii* (right) appreciates a well-drained soil

Daphne × burkwoodii   Semi-evergreen bush, 3 ft (1 m) tall and across, with pale pink, sweetly scented flowers. Sun or light shade.

Exochorda × macrantha 'The Bride'   Forms a low mound, to 2½–3 by 5 ft (0.8 × 1.5 m). Massed, pure white flowers with large papery petals contrast well with the fresh green, new leaves. Sun or light shade (see p.26).

Magnolia stellata   Dwarf rounded shrub, usually only 3 ft (1m) high and wide, but with time capable of attaining 10–13 by 6½–10 ft (3–4 × 2–3 m). Fragrant, pure white flowers with strap-like petals are carried on bare branches. The petals are easily bruised by frost, so shelter the plant from early morning sun. Sun or light shade (see p.26).

Osmanthus delavayi   Small, stiff, glossy green, evergreen leaves hidden by an abundance of very fragrant, pure white flowers. Slow growing, in ten years 3 by 2¼ ft (1 × 0.7 m), but may if unpruned attain 10–20 ft (3–6 m). Prune to control shape as required after flowering. Sun to reasonably deep shade. O. × burkwoodii, more vigorous and hardier in cold districts.

Paeonia delavayi (peony)   Suckering shrub, 3–5 ft (1–1.5 m) high and wide. Large single flowers, varying from yellow to crimson and, in the best forms, deep blood-red with golden anthers. Handsome, deeply dissected leaves up to 1¼ ft (0.4 m) long. Sun. Any well-drained soil.

Pieris taiwanensis   The best pieris for flowers, being loaded with racemes of pure white urn-shaped blooms held horizontally. New foliage is bronze-coloured. Makes a small, rounded, evergreen bush, 3–5 ft (1–1.5 m) tall and across. Prune only occasionally to control shape. Light shade. Acid soils only.

Prunus tenella 'Fire Hill'   Dwarf almond forming a spreading bush with erect stems, 4 ft (1.2 m) high and wide. Last year's shoots carry masses of rosy red flowers. Sun or light shade.

Rhododendron 'Bluebird'   Compact evergreen, 1½ ft (0.5 m) tall and across, with many rich violet-blue flowers hiding small, fragrant, somewhat yellowish green leaves (see also *Rhododendron*, p.35, for cultivation requirements).

R. calostrotum 'Gigha'   Rounded evergreen bush, 2–3 × 3 ft (0.6–1 × 1 m), with small grey-green leaves. Covers itself with deep claret-red flowers.

'Elizabeth' (left), one of the finest smaller rhododendron hybrids, was raised at Bodnant in North Wales; the lovely red flower buds of *Viburnum carlesii* 'Diana' (right) are borne throughout winter before opening in spring

R. 'Elizabeth'   Spreading evergreen, 3 by 4 ft (1 × 1.2 m), taller in shade, with large scarlet bell flowers and medium green leaves. Protect from early morning sun. R. 'Elisabeth Hobbie' and R. 'Scarlet Wonder', similar, but lower.

R. impeditum   Domed dwarf bush, 1 by 1½ ft (0.3 × 0.5 m), which will knit together to give effective evergreen groundcover. Tiny fragrant grey-green leaves, bronze over winter. Flowers pale purplish blue (see p.13).

R. williamsianum   Choice mound-forming evergreen, 3 by 6½ ft (1 × 2 m). Rounded leaves flushed bronze and maturing to dark green with a glaucous underside. Flowers, raised above the dense foliage, are soft rosy red bells 2 in. (5 cm) in diameter.

Ribes speciosum   Ornamental gooseberry, nearly evergreen, spiny and open branched, 5 ft (1.5 m) high and wide. Exquisite fuchsia-like red flowers hang beneath spreading shoots; these can be hit by late frosts. Prune by removing older shoots after flowering. Sun or light shade (see p.24).

Skimmia japonica   Evergreen growing to 3 by 4 ft (1 × 1.2 m), whose glossy leaves are aromatic when crushed. Grown for the very fragrant flowers, particularly on male plants such as 'Rubella', and for the large red berries, produced on female plants like 'Foremanii' when the two sexes are grown together. In 'Rubella', the flower buds are red, giving the bush a reddish hue over winter, and open to pink. Sun or light shade (see p.29).

Spiraea 'Arguta'   Rounded bush, 6½ ft (2 m) tall and wide. Pure white flowers on twiggy shoots of previous summer. Prune by removing old shoots. Sun.

Viburnum carlesii 'Diana'   Slowly develops a rounded, somewhat open habit, 5 ft (1.5 m) tall and across. Richly scented flowers borne in clusters formed the previous autumn, red in bud, opening to pale pink. Sun or light shade.

Weigela middendorffiana   Grows to 4 by 2½ ft (1.2 × 0.8 m) and has a buff-coloured bark. Flowers sulphur-yellow flecked with orange. Requires some shelter against spring frosts in cold gardens. Prune to remove old shoots after flowering. Sun or light shade.

EARLY SUMMER FLOWERS – LATE MAY TO JUNE

Buddleia alternifolia   Spreading, with weeping branches and shoots of the previous summer clothed with dense clusters of lilac-purple, tubular, fragrant flowers. Often recommended as a small weeping tree trained on to a single stem, eventually 10–20 ft (3–6 m) tall. However, if pruned immediately after flowering, to shape and remove old wood, a shrub 3–5 ft (1–1.5 m) high will result. Leaves dull green and glaucous beneath, silvery in 'Argentea' (see p.6).

B. globosa   Golden yellow, sweetly scented flowers in small rounded orange-like heads and long, matt green, lance-shaped leaves, evergreen except in severe winters. Makes an open rounded bush 10–13 ft (3–4 m) high and will regrow vigorously from cutting back; normal pruning should consist only of removing crowded old branches when flowering has ceased. Full sun (see p.32).

Ceanothus 'Blue Mound'   Dense domed evergreen 2 ft (0.6 m) tall, with mid-blue flowers (see p.12 and also *Ceanothus*, p.37, for cultivation requirements).

Clematis chrysocoma   Soft pink flowers in prodigious number, with an intermittent flush from August on. A climber to 26 ft (6 m), but can be cut back hard after flowering in early summer and allowed to clamber over medium-sized shrubs without smothering them. Sun to light shade.

Convolvulus cneorum   Shrubby bindweed, but not at all invasive, which must have a sheltered, rather dry position in full sun to flourish. Evergreen bush, 2 by 2½ ft (0.6 × 0.8 m), with a silvery appearance owing to silky hairs on the leaves. Large trumpet flowers, white tinged with pink with a yellow base, carried into August. Prune to remove untidy shoots in spring. Any well-drained soil (see p.24).

Deutzia   Reliable shrubs with fragrant flowers produced in small clusters along last year's shoots. New growths can be susceptible to spring frosts. They thrive on all soils in full sun or very light shade. After flowering, the older shoots should be removed to encourage strong long new growths.

D. × elegantissima 'Rosealind'   Forms rounded bush, 3–4 ft (1–1.2 m) high and wide, with deep carmine flowers. *D. × rosea* 'Carminea', flowers rose-carmine in bud, fading on opening (see p.32).

D. 'Magicien'   Grows to 6½ by 4 ft (2 × 1.2 m). Flowers large, pink tinted with a white edge and purple-streaked reverse. 'Mont Rose', rose-pink flowers with a deeper tint. *D. scabra* 'Candidissima', pure white, double flowers.

Elaeagnus umbellata   Rich fragrance of the flowers is detectable from several yards away, although these are small, creamy white and actually rather lost against the silvery foliage. Mature leaves bright green above and silvery beneath. Fruits orange-red. Forms bush, 10 ft (3 m) high and across, but can be restrained by pruning. Sun or light shade.

Genista lydia   A broom which has very wiry, green, pendulous shoots and fleeting leaves. Small arching plant, 2 by 2½ ft (0.6 × 0.8 m), with bright yellow flowers. Very effective at the front of a border or at the top of a sunny wall. Prune only into green shoots. Sun. Any well-drained soil.

Hebe   Evergreens with dense opposite leaves. Not particular about soil, apart from needing good drainage, but often damaged by severe winters and tend to be short-lived. They do not like pruning and should only ever be cut back to wood which is still green and leafy.

H. hulkeana (New Zealand lilac)   Sprawling shrub, 3 by 6½ ft (1 × 2 m) and the most spectacular hebe for flowers. These are small, delicate lavender or lilac, carried in enormous panicles at the ends of the shoots. Succeeds best against a sunny wall with good drainage.

H. pinguifolia 'Pagei'   Low shrub, 1 by 3 ft (0.3 × 1 m), with abundant white flowers. Perhaps its chief merit is the persistent, glaucous blue foliage.

Kalmia latifolia (calico bush)   Rhododendron-like plant with glossy evergreen foliage and beautiful saucer-shaped flowers, pink or red depending on cultivar.

Above: 'Kiwi' and other forms of *Leptospermum scoparium* thrive in the warmer southwestern counties of Britain

Below: *Poncirus trifoliata*, known as the Japanese bitter orange, is hardy and easily grown

Above: the free-flowering 'Goldfinger', one of many hybrids of the versatile *Potentilla fruticosa*

Below: *Rhododendron yakushimanum* is one of the most desirable small species and will even withstand full sun

Moist acid soil with light shade. Slow-growing, 5 ft (1.5 m) high and broad (see p.30).

Kolkwitzia amabilis 'Pink Beauty' Broad rounded bush, approximately 6 ft (1.8 m) tall and wide. Flowers on spur shoots produced off last season's growths, each spur terminating in a cluster of bell-shaped pink blooms. The fruits are curiously bristly and the leaves turn pinkish in autumn. Prune after flowering to replace three-year-old shoots. Sun or light shade.

Leptospermum scoparium (manuka, tea tree) Very twiggy dense evergreen, 8 ft (2.5 m) high, although with time in mild areas will make a small tree. Grown for beauty of the white flowers, which smother the foliage. Small evergreen leaves are aromatic if bruised. Not long-lived in most gardens, needing either the shelter of other plants or a position at the base of a wall. Full sun. 'Kiwi', low-growing with dark red, single flowers and bronze-tinted leaves (see p.41). 'Nicholsii', bright crimson flowers and bronze-red leaves. 'Red Damask', flowers fully double, deep cherry-red. 'Snow Flurry', white double flowers.

Lonicera syringantha Elegant plant, 3–5 by 5 ft (1–1.5 × 1.5 m), with fragrant, soft lilac flowers. Sun or light shade. Like other shrubby honeysuckles, deserves to be more widely used in gardens.

Poncirus trifoliata Unusual slow-growing relative of the lemon, 6½ ft (2 m) high and across, with strongly spined, matt green shoots. Sweetly scented 2 in. (5 cm) white flowers produced before the trifoliate leaves from axils of the spines, followed by bitter oranges with thick wrinkled skin. Sun or light shade (see p.41).

Potentilla (cinquefoil) Small shrubs valued for the length of the flowering season, from late May into early autumn. They grow on a wide range of soils in full sun or light shade and make excellent hedges. Young plants can be cut back to ground level, in older plants only old shoots should be removed. They have a peeling bark.

P. davurica 'Manchu' White flowers and grey-green foliage. Forms a spreading dwarf bush, 2–3 by 3 ft (0.6–1 × 1 m).

P. fruticosa Domed spreading plant, usually 3–4 by 3–5 ft (1–1.2 × 1–1.5 m), but only 2 ft (0.6 m) high in 'Sunset'. Most selections have yellow flowers, such as 'Elizabeth', 'Goldfinger' and 'Katherine Dykes'. 'Sunset', flowers deep orange to brick red. 'Vilmoriniana', cream-coloured flowers. 'Red Ace', glowing red flowers, better in light shade.

Rhododendron yakushimanum Slowly forms a rounded evergreen bush, 3 by 5 ft (1 × 1.5 m), with glossy, dark green leaves felted and richly coloured beneath. In bud the flowers are deep pink, paling as they open to white, carried in rounded trusses (see also *Rhododendron*, p.35, for cultivation requirements).

Japanese azaleas Low-growing evergreen bushes, 3–5 by 5 ft (1–1.5 × 1.5 m), which give an overwhelming display when covered in the large flowers. They need light shade and can be trimmed after flowering to prevent them getting too large and leggy. Selections available include 'Hinodegiri', crimson-scarlet flowers with deep coloured throat; 'Hinomayo', phlox-pink; and 'Palestrina', white.

Deciduous azaleas Bushes 3–6½ by 5 ft (1–2 × 1.5 m), with good autumn foliage colours. Sun or light shade. Among the many hybrids are 'Gibraltar', flowers dark red in bud opening to flame-orange with a yellow flash; 'Homebush', rose-madder, semi-double, in very neat rounded trusses; 'Klondyke', orange-gold with a red tint; 'Koster's Brilliant Red', glowing orange-red; and 'Persil', white with orange flare.

Rosa (rose) Hybrid tea and floribunda roses are grown in nearly all gardens, but are in many ways less suitable as shrubs for general use – and more demanding of attention – than the species, climbers and old-fashioned varieties. These thrive on all soils, although doing less well on shallow soils over chalk, require very little pruning, except to remove old wood, and will grow in sun or light shade.

R. elegantula (R. farreri) **'Persetosa'** Rounded bush up to 6½ ft (2 m) high, with masses of small pink flowers displayed against dainty fern-like foliage and small, bright red hips.

R. pimpinellifolia (Scotch or burnet rose) Low, suckering, very thorny shrub, up to 3 ft (1 m) high, especially suited to dry soils. Pale pink or creamy white flowers succeeded by black fruits.

R. xanthina 'Canary Bird' Large, fragrant, single, deep canary-yellow flowers carried for a month and repeated later in the year. Fresh green fern-like foliage. Makes a bush 6½ ft (2 m) high and across, almost devoid of prickles. R. 'Helen Knight', similar, with clear yellow saucer-shaped flowers and smaller leaves; grows 3–5 ft (1–1.5 m) tall.

Rosmarinus officinalis (rosemary) Erect dense evergreen, 6½ by 5 ft (2 × 1.5 m). Narrow leaves grey-green or green and white-felted beneath. Sun. Any well-drained soil. 'Severn Sea', brilliant blue flowers, arching habit, 2 ft (0.6 m) tall.

Rubus 'Beneden' Large white dog-rose flowers, faintly scented, on the previous season's shoots and fresh green, palmately lobed leaves. Makes a bush 6½ ft (2 m) tall and broad. Prune by removing old wood after flowering. Sun to moderate shade.

Syringa (lilac) Cultivars of common lilac generally offered will grow into small trees, but the following are very attractive and unusual shrubs. They need well-drained soil, full sun or very light shade and protection from frost. Do not prune except to control size.

S. microphylla 'Superba' Small oval leaves and a mass of fragrant, rosy pink flowers, mainly in May but intermittently until October. Grows to 5 by 3 ft (1.5 × 1 m) (see p.20).

S. × persica Spreading rounded bush, 3–5 by 5–6½ ft (1–1.5 × 1.5–2 m), with lilac-coloured flowers, white in 'Alba'.

Viburnum plicatum 'Mariesii' Spreading bush, 3–5 by 5–6½ ft (1–1.5 × 1.5–2 m), with abundant white flowers borne above the tiered foliage and leaves changing dull crimson in autumn. 'Pink Beauty', narrower in habit with flowers turning pink as they age. 'Rowallane', similar to 'Mariesii', but more reliable in production of bright red fruits. Sun or light shade.

Wisteria sinensis Climber capable of reaching 70 ft (20 m) up an oak tree, but can be grown against a house wall or trained as free-standing shrub. Large trusses of fragrant, deep lilac flowers hang below branches, with attractive pinnate leaves. Prune by shortening long whippy shoots to 6 in. (15 cm) in August and to two to three buds after leaf fall. Full sun. W. floribunda 'Macrobotrys', racemes of flowers up to 3 ft (1 m) long.

MIDSUMMER FLOWERS – JUNE TO JULY

Abutilon × suntense Erect shrub, 6½–10 by 3–5 ft (2–3 × 1–1.5 m), needing a sheltered site or warm sunny wall. Palmate, felted, grey leaves and masses of saucer-shaped flowers carried over a long period from midsummer on. Sun or light shade. Any well-drained soil. 'Jermyns', clear dark mauve flowers. 'Geoffrey Gorer' and 'White Charm', white.

Buddleia davidii (butterfly bush) Can be grown as a small tree, but is usually coppiced (i.e. pruned to ground level or a short stem) in March to produce long flowering shoots from July onwards; treated like this, it reaches 5–10 by 5–6½ ft (1.5–3 × 1.5–2 m). Flowers richly scented and attractive to butterflies. Seedlings have inferior flowers, and named clones should always be used, such as 'Black Knight', with dark violet flowers, and 'Royal Red', red-purple. Pruning is not essential and unpruned plants will flower earlier, with more numerous, smaller trusses. Sun or light shade.

Calycanthus floridus Grows to 5 ft (1.5 m) high and wide, with reddish purple flowers, very strongly scented. The leaves, wood and bark all have a camphor-like fragrance if bruised. Sun to moderate shade.

Above: 'Canary Bird', the commonest representative in gardens of *Rosa xanthina*, is a fine arching shrub

Below: *Viburnum plicatum* 'Rowallane' is more moderate in growth than 'Mariesii'

Above: the rock roses, including *Cistus* × *lusitanicus* 'Decumbens', are tolerant of wind and coastal exposure and happy on chalk soils

Below: the pink broom of New Zealand, *Notospartium carmichaeliae*, should survive most winters once established

Cistus (rock or sun rose) Evergreen shrubs needing full sun and tolerating dry sites. They cannot be pruned effectively and are short-lived, although very attractive. Large showy flowers open for a single morning, dropping the petals in the afternoon, but are produced in such numbers as to prolong the display. Any well-drained soil.

C. laurifolius White flowers with yellow boss of stamens carried from June to August. Upright shrub, 6½ by 3–5 ft (1 × 1–1.5 m), with a peeling purple bark. The hardiest species.

C. × lusitanicus 'Decumbens' Spreading bush, 3 by 5 ft (1 × 1.5 m). Flowers have white petals with basal crimson-purple blotch and central boss of golden stamens, borne from June into September.

C. × purpureus Grey-green aromatic leaves and large flowers with reddish pink petals and chocolate blotch. Not reliably hardy. Grows to 4 by 5 ft (1.2 × 1.5 m).

C. 'Silver Pink' Hardy form having long clusters of silver-pink flowers with golden stamens. Prefers richer soil than most rock roses. Grows to 2¼ by 3–5 ft (0.7 × 1–1.5 m).

Escallonia Evergreen shrubs which tolerate a wide range of soils and also maritime conditions. Many are not fully hardy. Flowering starts in June on last year's shoots and continues into autumn on current season's growths. They may be pruned to shape immediately after flowering, especially if grown against a wall or as a hedge. Unpruned, they grow 5–8 ft (1.5–2.5 m) tall. Sun to light shade.

E. 'Apple Blossom' Pink and white flowers. 'Donard Star', rose-pink flowers and larger, dark glossy green leaves. 'Edinensis', rose-pink flowers.

E. rubra 'Woodside' Smaller-growing, with a rounded habit, up to 2 ft (0.6 m) high, and rosy crimson flowers. Inclined to throw up vigorous shoots which should be removed.

Hebe armstrongii Yellow ochre-coloured whip-like shoots covered with small scale-leaves, forming a bush 1½ by 2 ft (0.5 × 0.6 m). Flowers in short white spikes (see also *Hebe*, p.40, for cultivation requirements).

H. 'Carl Teschner' Low mound, 8 in. by 2½ ft (0.2 × 0.8 m). Small leaves and violet flowers with a white throat.

Ligustrum sinense 'Pendulum' Rounded bush 5–6½ by 8 ft (1.5–2 × 2.5 m), with hanging shoots and large numbers of very fragrant, white flowers. Sun to light shade.

Lonicera caprifolium An early-flowering honeysuckle with very fragrant, creamy white flowers. Climber, growing 13–16½ ft (4–5 m) high. Sun or light shade.

Notospartium carmichaeliae Graceful arching habit, 4 ft (1.2 m) high, with lilac-pink pea flowers on leafless green shoots. May be killed by severe winters when young and needs well-drained soil. Full sun.

Olearia nummulariifolia Rounded evergreen bush, 5 ft (1.5m) high, with small thickly set, yellow-green leaves and scented white daisy flowers. Sun.

Rhododendron viscosum (swamp honeysuckle) Deciduous azalea producing very strongly scented, white or pink flowers which are sticky outside. Grows to 6½ ft (2 m) tall. Sun or light shade. Acid soils only, tolerating wet ones.

Rosa 'Buff Beauty' Hybrid musk rose with double apricot-yellow tea-scented flowers borne in successive flushes. Grows to 6 ft (1.8 m) tall and has coppery brown young foliage. May be hard pruned in spring or allowed to grow over large shrubs or small trees (see also *Rosa*, p.43, for cultivation requirements).

R. 'Maiden's Blush' Old-fashioned variety making a bush 4 ft (1.2 m) high, with healthy grey-green foliage. Flowers blush-pink, sweetly scented and very double. Prune out old shoots only.

R. rugosa 'Fru Dagmar Hastrup' Low-growing form of Ramanas rose, attaining 3 ft (1 m) high. Single flowers vivid pink in bud, opening to rose-pink, followed by large crimson edible hips rich in vitamin C. It suckers and is excellent for hedging.

Can be cut down to ground level in spring and will still flower by midsummer. Especially useful on sandy soils.

R. virginiana Small suckering rose 2 ft (0.6 m) high. Bright pink flowers, giving way to small rounded red fruits, and leaves also turning a fine colour in autumn. Good on sandy soils.

Salvia officinalis 'Icterina' Form of common sage with fragrant leaves variegated with yellow and light green. Evergreen, growing to 2 by 2½ ft (0.6 × 0.8 m). Sun. Any, especially light, soils.

Santolina chamaecyparissus (cotton lavender) Low bush, 1¼ by 2½ ft (0.4 × 0.8 m), with silvery evergreen foliage deeply cut as in filigree lace. Flowers are attractive yellow buttons. Flowering plants, however, lose their shapeliness; for maximum foliage effect, hard prune in April to promote vigorous leaf growth. Sun. Any, especially light, soils.

LATE SUMMER FLOWERS – JULY TO SEPTEMBER

Abelia × grandiflora Graceful shrub, 5 ft (1.5 m) high and wide, with bright green, evergreen foliage. Softly fragrant flowers carried on current season's growth from July into October, white tinged pale pink. Full sun. In coldest districts, place against a wall. 'Francis Mason', golden yellow foliage.

Aesculus parviflora Shrubby suckering horse chestnut, forming rounded clump 5–6½ by 10–13 ft (1.5–2 × 3–4 m). Leaves have five palmate leaflets, turning good colours in autumn. Flowers in glowing white candles 8–12 in. (20–30 cm) long. Sun to light shade.

Callistemon citrinus 'Splendens' Evergreen shrub, 3–5 by 5 ft (1–1.5 × 1.5 m), suitable for mild areas or set against a wall in full sun. Brilliant scarlet bottle-brush flowers. The leaves are lemon-scented when crushed. Not for chalk soils.

Calluna vulgaris (heather, ling) Native evergreen shrub, low and spreading, up to 1½ ft (0.5 m) high. Available in numerous forms, useful for both flowers and foliage. Prune by clipping after flowering. Sun or light shade. Acid soils only. 'Blazeaway', lilac-mauve flowers and green foliage which turns red in winter. 'Darkness', deep rose-purple flowers. 'Peter Sparkes', double pink. Gold foliage forms include 'Beoley Gold', 'Gold Haze' and 'Serlei', all with white flowers.

Caryopteris × clandonensis 'Heavenly Blue' Low-growing, up to 2½ ft (0.8 m) tall, with deep blue flowers. Prune to ground level in spring. Sun. Any well-drained soil.

Ceratostigma willmottianum Grows 2½ by 2 ft (0.8 × 0.6 m), with the leaves turning red in autumn. Bright blue flowers from July into October. Prune to ground level in spring (if winter cold has not done so!). Full sun. Dry well-drained soils.

Clematis vernayi (*C. orientalis*) (orange peel clematis) Climber flowering on current year's shoots. The yellow flowers have thick fleshy "petals", likened to orange peel, and are succeeded by silky seedheads. The greyish leaves are deeply cut. If left unpruned it will grow to 20 ft (6 m), if cut to ground in late winter it will reach 10–13 ft (3–4 m). Sun to light shade.

Clerodendron trichotomun var. fargesii Large rounded shrub, 8 ft (2.5 m) high. Fragrant white star-shaped flowers, followed by porcelain-blue berries set off by persistent crimson sepals. Sun or light shade.

Clethra alnifolia (sweet pepper bush) Reaches 5 by 3 ft (1.5 × 1 m). Flowers are strongly fragrant in erect, creamy white, 6 in. (15 cm) sprays. Prune by removing older stems in winter. Light to moderate shade. Moist lime-free soils. 'Rosea', pink in bud.

Cotinus coggygria (smoke bush) With time, forms a sprawling bush 10–13 ft (3–4 m) tall, with rounded green leaves turning brilliant red in autumn. Flowers in large clusters, attractive for their many slender silky-haired stalks which start pale

Above: the decorative hips of *Rosa rugosa* 'Fru Dagmar Hastrup' (left);
Ceratostigma willmottianum (right) contributes a welcome blue in late
summer

Below: *Callistemon citrinus* 'Splendens' (left), an eye-catching feature;
the conspicuous seedheads of *Clematis vernayi* (right)

The smoke bush, *Cotinus coggygria*, makes the most impressive display of flowers if the soil is not too rich

flesh colour and become smoky grey by autumn. Prune to restrict size. Sun or light shade. 'Royal Purple', purple foliage.

Daboecia cantabrica Evergreen heath, up to 1½ ft (0.5 m) tall. The flowers are pendent bells in erect terminal racemes, white in 'Alba', deep purple in 'Atro-purpurea'. Prune by clipping to remove spent flower heads. Sun or light shade. Acid soils only.

Desfontainea spinosa Evergreen, 5 by 4 ft (1.5 × 1.2 m), with spiny shiny holly-like leaves. Large tubular flowers, with a crimson scarlet tube and yellow lobes. Needs a sheltered position. Light shade. Moist lime-free soil (see p.22).

Deutzia monbeigii Grows to 4 ft (1.2 m) tall and across. The small leaves are white beneath, giving a grey tone to the plant. Carries clusters of glistening white star-shaped flowers (see also *Deutzia*, p.40, for cultivation requirements).

Erica (heather) *E. cinerea*, *E. tetralix* and *E. vagans* and their forms are spreading evergreen shrubs with bell-shaped white, pink or crimson flowers. Like *Calluna* and *Daboecia*, they should be planted in groups, at about 5 to 10 plants per square yard. They will grow 1 ft (0.3 m) tall, but are best clipped after flowering to prevent them getting leggy. Sun. Acid soils only.

Fremontodendron 'California Glory' Only hardy for a few average winters with the protection of a warm sunny wall, but well worth trying. Evergreen erect shrub, 10–13 by 5–6½ ft (3–4 × 1.5–2 m), with large, bright lemon yellow flowers over an ex-tended period. South-facing aspect. Any well-drained soil.

Hebe 'Autumn Glory' Succession of intense violet-blue flowers until stopped by frost. Leaves glossy green with purple tinge. Makes an erect spreading bush, 2 by 2½ ft (0.6 × 0.8 m) (see p.52 and also *Hebe*, p.40, for cultivation requirements).

H. × franciscana 'Blue Gem' Hardier than most hebes, forming a compact dome-shaped bush, 2 ft (0.6 m) high and broad, with fresh green leaves and bright blue flowers.

H. 'Great Orme' Displays bright pink flowers against large spear-shaped leaves. Compact bush, 2½ ft (0.8 m) tall and across.

Hibiscus syriacus Grows 10–13 ft (3–4 m) high, but easily restricted by pruning in late winter. Produces hollyhock-like flowers on current season's shoots. Full sun. Any well-drained soil. 'Blue Bird', bright blue flowers up to 3 in. (8 cm) in diameter. 'Diana', white (see p.30). 'Woodbridge', rich pink.

Hydrangea arborescens 'Annabelle' Low-growing shrub, 3 by 5 ft (1 × 1.5 m), which carries very large heads of glistening white flowers. Needs moist soil, but will take full sun to moderate shade. Prune by removing spent flowers.

H. paniculata Large shrub or can be grown into a small tree, 13 ft (4 m) or more high. May be hard pruned in late winter to produce larger panicles of flowers, which are in triangular heads and creamy white, ageing to pinkish. 'Praecox', first to flower in July, followed by 'Grandiflora', then 'Tardiva' in September and early October.

H. serrata 'Preziosa' Small-flowered but very hardy hortensia hydrangea, growing to 4 by 3 ft (1.2 × 1 m). Flowers salmon-pink, later warm red, and foliage attractively tinged purple when young. Sun or light shade (see p.52).

Hypericum forrestii Upright evergreen or semi-evergreen bush, 3–5 by 3 ft (1–1.5 × 1 m). Can be hard pruned in spring and will produce large golden yellow flowers, followed by bronzy red young fruits. Sun. Any well-drained soil. H. 'Hidcote', more compact rounded bush with a longer flowering season until cut by autumn frosts, but rarely fruits.

Indigofera heterantha Develops luxuriant feathery or pinnate foliage on long wand-like shoots, with rosy purple pea flowers. Cut back to ground level in spring, when it will reach 5 ft (1.5 m) high and wide. Sun. Any well-drained soil (see p.53).

Lavandula angustifolia (lavender) Dwarf evergreen shrub, 2½ ft (0.8 m) tall and across, with silvery grey foliage and fragrant blue flowers. Sun. Any well-drained soil. 'Hidcote', smaller form with purple flowers.

Lonicera × brownii 'Dropmore Scarlet' Vigorous climbing honeysuckle, 10–13 ft (3–4 m) high, with clusters of bright scarlet, tubular flowers from July into October. Sun or light shade.

Olearia × haastii Rounded shrub, 4 ft (1.2 m) high and wide, with small evergreen leaves, grey beneath. Fragrant white flowers in large daisy-like heads. No pruning necessary except for hedges. Sun.

O. macrodonta (New Zealand holly) Large sage-green spined leaves, richly silvered beneath. Evergreen, 6½ ft (2 m) tall and broad, with fragrant white flowers in large clusters. Less reliably hardy, but excellent for coastal situations. Sun or light shade.

Senecio compactus Crinkled leaves felted pure white beneath and yellow daisy flowers. Compact evergreen shrub, 3 by 5–6½ ft (1 × 1.5–2 m). Cut back in spring to two to three buds to control size. Sun or light shade. Any well-drained soil. S. 'Sunshine', better flowers but grey-green leaves.

S. scandens Strong-growing climber up to 10–13 ft (3–4 m), with masses of yellow daisy flowers. Slightly tender and needs a sheltered site in sun. It can be cut back hard in spring, if not killed back by winter cold.

Solanum crispum 'Glasnevin' Climber with potato flowers of rich purple-blue with yellow centres over a long period. Can be pruned back in spring and will reach 13–20 ft (4–6 m). Requires a sheltered position in full sun (see p.53).

Spiraea japonica Grows into a rounded shrub, 5 by 6½ ft (1.5 × 2 m), with rose-pink flowers. Prune by removing surplus old shoots in spring and shortening those remaining. Sun or light shade. 'Goldflame' (S. × bumalda 'Goldflame'), new foliage golden yellow with bronzy red tips, becoming greener with age; needs moist soil (see p.17). 'Little Princess', mound-forming, 3 × 6½ ft (1 × 2 m), with rose-crimson flowers.

Above: *Hebe* 'Autumn Glory' needs a well-drained soil and flowers almost continuously from midsummer on

Below: like all hydrangeas, *H. serrata* 'Preziosa' prefers a moist soil doing well in sun or semi-shade

Above: *Indigofera heterantha* remains in flower throughout summer and autumn

Below: *Solanum crispum* 'Glasnevin', a vigorous semi-evergreen climber which flourishes in chalky soils

AUTUMN EFFECT

The following shrubs produce decorative fruits, which often persist over winter. Several other shrubs are valuable for autumn flowers (see pp.48–51) or foliage (see pp.59–62).

Callicarpa bodinieri 'Profusion' Erect shrub, 6½ by 4 ft (2 × 1.2 m). Purple-blue fruits in clusters along the previous year's shoots make a striking display after leaf fall and remain into winter. They are preceded by mauve-pink flowers in July and August. Prune to remove old stems. Sun or light shade.

Cotoneaster Versatile shrubs for sun or light shade, tolerating wide range of soils.

C. bullatus Grows to 8 by 6½ ft (2.5 × 2 m) and gives brilliant fiery autumn colours from the large corrugated leaves. Berries bright red.

C. conspicuus Spreading mound, 3 by 5–6½ ft (1 × 1.5–2 m), with small evergreen foliage and showy white flowers in early summer. The abundant, bright red, juicy berries, which may persist until Easter, are the best feature.

C. franchetti Oval orange-scarlet berries lasting until Christmas or beyond. Small evergreen sage-green leaves and a graceful arching habit, 6½ ft (2 m) high and across.

C. horizontalis Spreading, with herring-bone pattern branches. Mainly grown as a wall shrub, reaching 6½–13 ft (2–4 m) or more; otherwise, forms a mound, 1½–3 by 5 ft (0.5–1 × 1.5 m). Berries scarlet and small glossy leaves which turn orange before falling.

C. lacteus Leathery oval evergreen leaves provide a foil for the milky white flowers in June and later for the long-lasting red fruits. Makes a shrub 10 ft (3 m) high and wide. Prune to control size.

Euonymus alatus 'Compacta' Mound-shaped bush, 2½ by 4 ft (0.8 × 1.2 m]. The foliage turns brilliant red in autumn and the twigs have curious corky wings. Sun or light shade.

Ilex cornuta Evergreen holly, 3 by 5 ft (1 × 1.5 m), with strangely shaped, glossy green leaves – rectangular, having scalloped margins and five spines. Berries red. Sun or light shade.

I. crenata 'Mariesii' Erect evergreen, 4 by 2½ ft (1.2 × 0.8 m), with black berries. Sun or light shade.

Pernettya mucronata Suckering evergreen shrub, 1½–3 by 3 ft (0.5–1 × 1 m) or more. Small white bell-shaped flowers followed, on female plants, by large white or coloured berries which remain over winter. One male plant must be planted to every 3 to 5 female ones. They associate well with heathers. Sun or light shade. Acid soils only. 'Bell's Seedling', red berries. 'Cherry Ripe', bright cherry-red ones (see p.18). 'Mother of Pearl', light pink berries. 'White Pearl', glistening white.

Ruscus aculeatus (butcher's broom) Evergreen member of the lily family. The "leaves" are modified shoots and on female plants carry flowers in the centre, giving large red berries in autumn. Suckering shrub, 1½ by 3 ft (0.5 × 1 m). Light to deep shade.

Sorbus reducta Dwarf suckering rowan, 3 by 1½–5 ft (1 × 0.5–1.5 m). Fruits pinky white and pinnate leaves turn bronze and purple before falling in autumn. Sun to light shade. Neutral to acid soils.

Symphoricarpos Useful shrubs with colourful berries which tolerate quite shady positions.

S. × chenaultii 'Hancock' Dwarf suckering plant, 2 by 8 ft (0.6 × 2.5 m), with pinkish purple berries. 'Magic Berry', abundant lilac-carmine berries, 4 ft (1.2 m) high and across. 'Mother of Pearl', arching habit, 5 ft (1.5 m) tall and wide, with white berries tinted pink.

Above: *Callicarpa bodinieri* 'Profusion' (left) does not need to be grown in groups to produce its unusual fruits; *Cotoneaster bullatus* (right), with its glistening red berries and attractive foliage, is an excellent species

Below: the bold evergreen foliage of *Viburnum davidii* is enhanced by the blue berries

Viburnum davidii Dense low mound, 2½ by 5 ft (0.8 × 1.5 m), although old plants may grow 5 ft (1.5 m) tall. Deep green, evergreen leaves have three prominent veins. Turquoise-blue berries which persist over winter are the main attraction. Plant two or more for pollination of female plants. Sun to moderate shade (see p.55).

WINTER EFFECT – DECEMBER TO FEBRUARY/MARCH

Chimonanthus praecox (winter sweet) Bushy shrub up to 8 ft (2.5 m) tall, often grown against a wall. Ivory to yellow flowers very pleasantly scented and borne over a long period. The leaves also have a spicy fragrance. Sun to light shade.

Cornus alba (dogwood) Grown mainly for pronounced red colour of the one-year-old shoots. Best if hard pruned to ground annually at end of March, then growing to 3–4 ft (1–1.2 m) high and wide. Sun to light shade. Any soil, especially wet ones. 'Elegantissima', green and silver variegated foliage. 'Spaethii', golden variegated foliage; both also have good barks.

C. stolonifera 'Flaviramea' Lemon-yellow winter shoots, going well with the red-stemmed dogwoods (see p.18).

Corylus avellana 'Contorta' (corkscrew hazel) Twisted and curled branches give an interesting winter silhouette, with yellow hanging catkins in February. Grows 6½–10 by 6½ ft (2–3 × 2 m). Tolerates full sun to moderate shade.

Daphne bholua Deciduous or semi-evergreen erect shrub, 5 by 3 ft (1.5 × 1 m), with a long succession of rose-purple richly scented flowers. Sun or light shade. 'Gurkha' and 'Jacqueline Postill', named forms.

Erica herbacea (E. carnea) (heath) Flowers from January to March and, unlike other heaths, will grow on all soils, including those on chalk. Spreading low shrub, 4–12 in. (10–30 cm) tall. Clip after flowering. Sun or light shade. Good forms are 'King George', early, from November, flowers carmine; 'Springwood White', best white; 'Springwood Pink', rose-pink; and 'Vivellii', deep red with dark bronze winter foliage. On acid soils, coloured foliage forms of Calluna vulgaris (see p.48) can also be used.

Garrya elliptica 'James Roof' Grown for the male catkins up to 14 in. (35 cm) long. Evergreen rounded shrub 10 ft high, but often grown against a wall, particularly in cold districts. Prune to control size after flowering. Sun or light shade. Good for north and east aspects.

Lonicera fragrantissima Shrubby honeysuckle growing 6 ft (1.8 m) tall and across, with cream-coloured strongly fragrant flowers. Red berries may follow in May. Sun to light shade.

Mahonia × media Bold-foliaged evergreen capable of forming a small tree after 15 to 20 years, but after ten years only 6½ by 5 ft (2 × 1.5 m). Leaves set in rosettes at tips of shoots, in which are carried fragrant yellow flowers from October until after Christmas. Sun to moderate shade. Good named forms include 'Lionel Fortescue', 'Buckland' and 'Charity'.

Rhododendron mucronulatum Erect semi-evergreen shrub, 5 ft (1.5 m) high, with delightful, bright rose-purple flowers. Needs siting where it will not be caught by morning sun, as the blossoms can be damaged by frost. Light to moderate shade. Acid soils only.

Sarcococca humilis Dense evergreen suckering shrub, 1½ by 3 ft (0.5 × 1 m). White flowers, richly scented, lead to black berries. Sun to moderate shade.

S. ruscifolia Erect evergreen bush, 4 by 3 ft (1.2 × 1 m), with crimson berries.

Viburnum farreri Starts flowering as the leaves drop in autumn and continues until February, depending upon weather. Flowers fragrant, pale pink in bud opening to white. Less showy in flower than V. × bodnantense forms, such as 'Deben' and 'Dawn', but superior for the erect habit with spreading branches, 6½ by 4 ft (2 × 1.2 m), and for the neat foliage with bronze new growths.

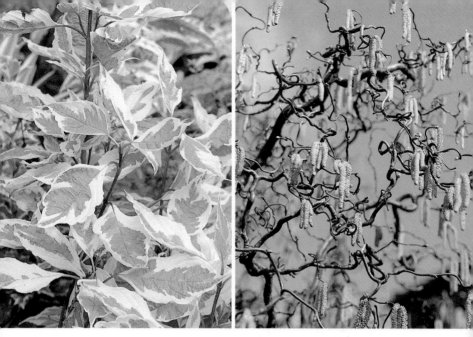

Above: *Cornus alba* 'Elegantissima' (left), a variegated form of the
dogwood which is less rampant than the species itself; the curious
corkscrew hazel, *Corylus avellana* 'Contorta' (right), was originally
discovered in a Gloucestershire hedgerow

Below: *Viburnum farreri*, still better known as *V. fragrans*, is a
favourite shrub for the winter garden

Above: the climbing *Actinidia kolomikta* should be pruned in winter

Below: *Berberis thunbergii* 'Atropurpurea Nana', a useful dwarf bush for massing or as a low hedge

YEAR-ROUND INTEREST

Shrubs grown primarily for the beauty of their foliage can provide colour, shape and texture throughout the year and several are also attractive in flower. Similarly, many of the flowering shrubs already described are useful for their decorative foliage.

Dwarf conifers also supply permanent interest and add an element of scale, grandeur or variety to a garden setting, particularly when associated with heathers and other rather flat plants or in a rock garden. They require no pruning and are suitable for full sun to light shade and any soil. (See also the Wisley handbooks, *Foliage plants* and *Dwarf and slow-growing conifers*.)

Abies nordmanniana 'Golden Spreader' Upright, normally flat-topped fir up to 3 ft (1 m) high, with dense, bright golden yellow foliage. Better sited in light shade, as in full sun the colour may be bleached; in deep shade it becomes greener.

A. lasiocarpa 'Compacta' Bright blue-grey foliage on a neat conical plant. Grows 3–4 ft (1–1.2 m) tall in ten years, eventually reaching 10–13 ft (3–4 m).

Acer palmatum 'Bloodgood' A superior selection of Japanese maple with rich red-purple leaves which retain colour well throughout summer, turning bright red before falling. Makes an upright rounded bush, 8 ft (2.5 m) high. Sun or light shade. Any soil, better in acid ones.

A. palmatum 'Dissectum' Bright green, deeply divided foliage. Forms a shapely rounded bush, 2 by 3 ft (0.6 × 1 m), and is well placed drooping over a low wall. The autumn colour is bronzy yellow (see p.9).

Actinidia kolomikta Climber up to 10–13 ft (3–4 m), with large leaves which become white flushed with pink on top half. The colour is stronger in full sun, but will take light shade. White flowers in June are slightly fragrant. Prune to restrain.

Artemisia 'Powis Castle' Dome, 2–3 by 3–4 ft (0.6–1 × 1–1.2 m), with silvery leaves which are deeply cut like lace filigree. Prune by cutting back to near ground level in spring. Sun.

Arundinaria murieliae Strong-growing but non-invasive bamboo. Forms rounded mop-head of rich green, nearly evergreen leaves on cluster of green or yellow stems, up to 10–13 ft (3–4 m) tall and across. Prune by removing old stems. Light to deep shade. Any moist soil.

Berberis thunbergii Barberry growing to 5 by 4 ft (1.5 × 1.2 m), with sealing wax red berries and brilliant autumn colours. Sun or light shade. 'Aurea', leaves yellow, becoming light green. 'Atropurpurea Nana', dwarf form 2 ft (0.6 m) high, with purple foliage. 'Red Chief', good wine red foliage on upright arching bush, 6 by 5 ft (1.8 × 1.5 m). 'Rose Glow', young leaves purple with silver-pink and rose mottling, becoming plain purple as they age (see p.15).

Cedrus deodora 'Golden Horizon' Spreading form of deodar cedar with golden foliage, 3 by 6½–10 ft (1 × 2–3 m). The foliage becomes more bluish green in shade.

Chamaecyparis pisifera 'Filifera Aurea' Long whip-like golden-yellow shoots pendulous at tips, forming an attractive mound, 3 by 4 ft (1 × 1.2 m), slowly increasing to 10–13 ft (3–4 m) tall.

Elaeagnus × ebbingei Evergreen bush, 10 ft (3 m) high and across, with leaves silvery beneath. Unusual for carrying the very fragrant pale flowers in October. Sun or light shade. Any except shallow chalk soil. 'Gilt Edge', leaves margined with gold. 'Limelight', leaves with large deep yellow centre. Remove all shoots which have reverted to pure green as soon as possible.

Euonymus fortunei Evergreen climber which has given rise to several small low-growing forms, 1 by 2–3 ft (0.3 × 0.6–1 m), making good groundcover with their

colourful foliage. Sun to deep shade. 'Emerald Gaiety', green leaves with silver variegation. 'Emerald 'n' Gold', gold-variegated foliage turning pinkish in winter. 'Silver Queen', creamy white-variegated.

Fothergilla major   Rounded bush to 3–5 ft (1–1.5 m) high and wide, with two conspicuous seasons of display – red, orange or yellow foliage in autumn and fragrant white bottle-brush flowers before the leaves in April and May. Light shade. Acid soils only (see also p.2).

Hedera algeriensis (*H. canariensis*) **'Gloire de Marengo'**   Large variegated leaves deep green in the centre, creamy white on the margins and silvery-grey in patches. A useful evergreen self-clinging climber for covering walls, sheds and trees. Sun or light shade (see p.9).

H. helix 'Conglomerata Erecta'   Non-clinging form of common ivy, with stiffly erect-growing shoots to 3 ft (1 m) high, making a low hummock, and evergreen leaves arranged in two rows. 'Congesta' is similar. 'Buttercup', vigorous climber with leaves of rich yellow, paling with age (see p.62). Sun to deep shade.

Juniperus horizontalis   Ground-hugging juniper growing no higher than 4–6 in. (10–15 cm), but covering 6½–10 ft (2–3 m) and particularly useful as a foil for dwarf bulbs or as low groundcover. 'Douglasii', foliage bright glaucous green in summer, developing a purplish tinge over winter. 'Wiltonii', glaucous blue leaves.

J. squamata 'Blue Carpet'   Foliage of intense steely blue, growing 1 by 3–6½ ft (0.3 × 1–2 m). 'Blue Star', similar in colour, remaining low and compact, 1 by 1½ ft (0.3 × 0.5 m).

Lonicera nitida 'Baggesen's Gold'   Shrubby evergreen honeysuckle with bright golden yellow leaves, becoming yellowish green in autumn, and dense arching habit, to 4 by 3 ft (1.2 × 1 m). Sun or light shade.

Nandina domestica (heavenly bamboo)   Unbranched erect stems 4 ft (1.2 m) tall, bearing rosettes of compound evergreen foliage. The leaves are crimson and scarlet when young and also in autumn. Small white flowers in large terminal clusters in June and July, followed by red berries. Sun to moderate shade.

Parthenocissus henryana   Vigorous climber up to 16½ by 10 ft (5 × 3 m), clinging by suction pads and tendrils. Leaves are bronzy dark green with silvery white veins, turning brilliant crimson before falling in autumn. Sun or light shade, best on north or east walls.

Photinia × fraseri 'Red Robin'   Brilliant red young foliage which matures to dark glossy green. Evergreen rounded bush up to 6½ ft (2 m) or more high, but can be pruned immediately after the leaves have matured to give a further flush of colour. Sun or light shade.

Pieris formosa 'Wakehurst'   Vivid red new leaves becoming dark green. When mature, erect or rounded evergreen shrub, 6 by 5 ft (1.8 × 1.5 m), with ivory-white flowers in April. Must have acid soil and shelter from late spring frosts, as growth starts early. Light shade. P. 'Forest Flame', similar with leaves turning through pink and creamy white as they age.

Pinus pumila 'Dwarf Blue'   Pine with long drooping blue-grey needles. Will form a flat-topped bush 1¼ by 1½ ft (0.4 × 0.5 m).

P. sylvestris 'Gold Coin'   Rounded bush reaching a maximum height of 3–6½ ft (1–2 m). Bluish needles turn bright golden during winter.

Rhamnus alaterna 'Argenteovariegata'   Develops into rounded bushy evergreen shrub, up to 8 ft (2.5 m) tall. Small glossy green leaves are mottled grey and margined with creamy white. Sun to deep shade.

Opposite: *Fothergilla major* has conspicuous flower spikes in spring, in addition to the beautifully coloured foliage in autumn

'Buttercup', the best yellow form of the common ivy, *Hedera helix*

Ribes sanguineum 'Brocklebankii'   Flowering currant, 3 ft (1 m) tall and broad, with golden yellow leaves and pink flowers. Prune by removing three-year-old shoots after flowering. Light to moderate shade.

Salix lanata   Willow with woolly, silvery green leaves, contrasting well with erect, yellowish grey catkins in spring. Makes low bush, 3 by 4 ft (1 × 1.2 m) Sun. Any moist soil.

Sambucus racemosa 'Plumosa Aurea'   Deeply dissected, golden leaves and white flowers giving rise to red berries. Grows to 6½ by 5 ft (2 × 1.5 m) or more. Prune to restrain. Sun or light shade.

Weigela florida 'Variegata'   Dense bush, 5 by 4 ft (1.5 × 1.2 m) with bright creamy white-margined leaves and pink flowers in June. Leave unpruned or remove three-year-old shoots after flowering. Sun or light shade.

W. praecox 'Variegata'   Similar, with scented rose-pink flowers in May.

Index of shrubs

Bold numbers refer to illustrations